MIGRATORY BIRDS
Mariana Oliver

TRANSLATED BY
Julia Sanches

**TRANSIT
BOOKS**

Published by Transit Books
2301 Telegraph Avenue, Oakland, California 94612
www.transitbooks.org

First published in Spanish as *Aves migratorias*
Copyright © Mariana Oliver, 2014
English translation copyright © Julia Sanches, 2021

"Özdamar's Tongue" first appeared in *Words Without Borders.*

ISBN: 978-1-945492-52-5 (paperback) | 978-1-945492-53-2 (ebook)
LIBRARY OF CONGRESS CONTROL NUMBER: 2021932621

COVER DESIGN
Anna Morrison

TYPESETTING
Justin Carder

DISTRIBUTED BY
Consortium Book Sales & Distribution
(800) 283-3572 | cbsd.com

Printed in the United States of America

9 8 7 6 5 4 3 2

 This project is supported in part by a grant from the National Endowment
for the Arts.

To Laura Flamand,
every day,
every light.

To my parents.

I.

MIGRATORY

BIRDS

Bill Lishman was turned down by every aviation school in Canada. No amount of enthusiasm will help if a runway and a field of grass look the same color. If a recessive gene is passed down through generations and settles in your X chromosome so that you can't tell red from green, you won't be working as a firefighter, a painter, or an electrician. If you can't tell a fresh apple skin from one that's too ripe, you won't be allowed to pilot planes. You'll have to watch them through the window, like birds.

Just like that, as he watched birds through the window, a young Bill Lishman looked down at his featherless skin and realized he envied their wings. So he decided to build himself a pair to amend his imperfect body. Before him, mankind had learned to fly by observing the movement of birds: the flight of birds and of planes is governed by the same principles. Wings are flat, aerodynamic surfaces that rely on the force of air; the

pressure above needs to be lesser and the pressure below greater. This is the key to defying gravity.

•

One advantage of growing up in the countryside is that any
backyard can be turned into your own practice runway. Bill
used to climb a hill every day, dragging behind him the other half of his body: a broad, delta-shaped canvas surface that
he strapped to his torso on reaching the summit. Fitted with
wings, he'd dash downhill and a gust of wind would lift him
from the earth. On a successful takeoff, the feeling of the
ground brushing his feet was first and last. His body graceful-
ly rose above the house where he'd grown up and above the
row of monochrome trees. Then came the inevitable descent,
when the body's weight doubles and the wings turn into painful prosthetics, cheap knockoffs.

Because his flights felt shorter and shorter and he was tired
of hauling his delta wing up the hill time and again, Bill added
an engine. By the late seventies, Bill Lishman had become a
pioneer of ultralight aviation.

•

Sometimes, out of the blue, you catch a glimpse of the future.
A moment of insight that disrupts the day-to-day, a revelation
that becomes impossible to shake off. In the middle of a practice

flight, Bill noticed he was no longer alone but encircled by a large flock of ducks migrating south. For a couple of minutes the speed of the birds and of the aircraft were one and the same, and together they traveled a short distance. It was like his body had multiplied. As he flew among the birds, Bill became one too. And even though he'd taught himself to pilot planes because he enjoyed solitude, the airborne company of those dusky-brown birds was an unexpected pleasure that made him feel less vulnerable.

•

He was Canadian and had an abundant, salt-and-pepper beard. His flight goggles left a crisp line around his eyes, beneath which sat a long and ruddy nose. They were talking about him on the news because he'd raised sixteen wild geese in his back-yard. He'd taught the geese how to eat and defend themselves, and that the first step to overcoming fear is balance. Journalists recounted with astonishment that Bill Lishman, in anticipation of winter, had led his geese along a southbound route to a place where the weather was less severe. He flew a thousand kilometers with them, from Ontario to Virginia.

Bill told himself when he got home that some trips can only ever be taken in one direction, that he would never see those geese again; after all, it's impossible to find the way back when there are no tracks to follow. He forgot that home is a route anchored in memory. The geese flew back the following spring. They returned to the place they'd left and even though they'd been changed by the trip, Bill could still tell them apart. Which is why people started calling him "Papa Goose."

•

Certain bird species are naïve. They leave their shells and entrust their lives to the first thing they come into contact with, be it their mother, their father, or any other living or mechanical thing. They follow them wherever they go and mimic their behavior to make them happy, which ensures their survival. This is similar to how children form bonds with their parents, and why they imitate their expressions and movements, and learn to use words and phrases they don't understand as though they were their own. Home is also a mirrored gesture.

A famous photograph illustrates this behavior. In it an elderly man walks through a field in shorts and a baggy shirt; he smokes a pipe and looks down at the ground, deep in thought. Behind him waddle a row of ducklings that seem like they're in a rush. The man is Konrad Lorenz, an Austrian zoologist who had dedicated his life to studying avian behavior. From the image it's clear that the ducks are following Lorenz, and yet the path he follows is hidden from sight. In most photographs of Lorenz, ducks keep him company.

•

Before their habitat was destroyed and their population was decimated by hunters, whooping cranes lived in North America and migrated south every year. By the 1940s, they were a species condemned to disappear, reduced to a series of photographs. A group of cranes was raised in captivity in a bid to save them, but the results fell short. Once they were reintroduced to the wild, the cranes were reluctant to breed and when they did, were unable to care for their colts. Come fall, they ignored their instinct to migrate and joined a group of sedentary birds; they didn't survive. In captivity, cranes never live beyond infancy.

·

Migration is one of the most fascinating behavioral patterns of certain bird species. An enduring need for repetition that compels them to travel great distances, even at risk to their lives. Hence the reason they fly in groups. In a flock, the bird that acts as guide and figurehead is also the one that breaks the wind, mitigating air resistance for the other birds. Day after day they swap positions and share the burden of their journey. Among migrating birds, permanence is an acceptance of death.

·

Some years ago, Bill Lishman joined a group of researchers whose goal was to save whooping cranes from extinction.

Someone reasoned that since Bill had led a flock of geese hundreds of kilometers and the geese had been able to find their way back, he might do the same for cranes. In captivity, the work starts before the cranes are born. Eggs are placed in incubators and the caregivers play a recording of an ultralight engine three times a day. When the chicks break through their shells, the first thing they see is a crane-shaped puppet that little by little teaches them basic things, like how to find food and regulate their sleep cycle. As soon as they sprout feathers, the cranes learn to fly with help from an ultralight painted in matching colors. Following the sounds they know best, they undertake the first migratory journey of their lives from Wisconsin to Florida. Home is also a recording from childhood, an implanted memory.

·

A man pilots a yellow ultralight across the sky. His name, Bill, Bill, Bill, is the last thing he hears before his feet take wing. All liftoffs are the same, he thinks, a ritual by which we become birds. As the body rises, the mind blots out all sounds and refashions them one by one, as if they existed in isolation. First heartbeat, then breath, then saliva moistening the throat; then the whoosh of air as the ultralight's wings break it into a white trail. Bill, Bill, Bill, his name echoes three times in his helmet. If they'd yelled out the name William, which is what his father used to call him, he thinks they'd only have managed to say it once. Though it's possible they'd have dragged out the vowels so that each syllable hovered in the air for as long as possible. Even though everything seems clearer to him from far away, he knows it's too late to glance down and take in everyone saying goodbye or the childish astonishment that lights up people's faces whenever they see a flying machine. From the distance where he is, all expression is beyond grasp.

As though sensing his thoughts or wanting to interrupt them, the flock behind him begins to whoop. Ever since he first heard them, Bill has had the feeling that whoever decided to call those birds whooping cranes had never flown beside them; way up high, their cries are of jubilation, not the dissonant celebration of a death by hunting. The cranes stretch out their legs and long necks as they fly, and the black edge on the mirror-side of their wings contrasts with the snow-white feathers above them. They grow larger and majestic when defying gravity. The cranes soar, charcoal strokes across the sky.

Bill smiles, having just realized that the cranes and the ultralight only look the same to his eyes. Anyone seeing him from below would think they were staring up at a peculiar-looking flock. They'd believe the cranes had lost their minds, trailing behind a big yellow bird.

II.

CAPPADOCIA

I

They must have arrived by horse, weapons in formation, ready for battle, like an orchestra waiting for the baton to rise. They're one fabric, a single organism marching in the same direction. Beneath their armor, hearts pound at full tilt and veins fire up with the knowledge that victory draws near. The men look like felines ready to descend on their prey. The whole city quakes. The thud of dry iron gallops against the earth, heralding their approach. What had been a murmur is now a clamor. Then silence. There is no screaming or crying, and there will be no spoils of war. Maybe the men were too preoccupied with their own shock to notice the expression of the person next to them, or of whoever had led the assault. All of them know that you can't win a battle when there is no enemy. The city before them is empty.

·

The men on horseback don't realize that the city they're look-ing for breathes safe and sound beneath their feet. They don't suspect there are masses below alert to their movements, wait-ing to see how long they will stay. Neither do they know that the ground they're standing on is also a cavern, or that it's made of centuries-old volcanic ash that had once bred its own root system, which extends into a tunnel, a church, and then a sta-ble, and finally a well.

•

At the behest of Emperor Theodosius, the writer Flavius Vege-tius Renatus left a meticulous record of Roman military prac-tices in his book *Epitoma rei militaris.* In it he collected the many strategies and techniques of the Roman army before their de-feat in Adrianople, highlighting their characteristic discipline and grandeur. There was a time when Vegetius's book was considered essential reading for any military strategist worth their salt. Yet the author had failed to explain how to conquer a city that has barricaded itself underground.

•

The underground city is an impenetrable burrow. The pocked millstone that blocks the entrance can only be opened from the inside. Some chambers are eighty-five meters below the sur-face. Thousands of people could survive down there with no shortage of water, oxygen, or food. Still, even though they had shelter, the absence of light made them sickly and tired, and they grew a little sadder and grayer every day. Their sightless troglodyte bodies aged before their time, their bones became soft and their joints weak, and they hunched under the weight of their flesh. Everyone knew that the longer they stayed underground, the harder it would be to live again above the surface.

•

The region of Cappadocia is in the heart of the Anatolian peninsula. Mountainous since the beginning of time, it is far from the influx of the Mediterranean, the waters of the Aegean, and the Dead Sea. The Taurus Mountains form a wall that binds the region in the south, sentencing the area to extreme temperatures. A historically important trade route, Cappadocia stands at the intersection between East and West. The whole of humanity has passed through here: Hittites, Armenians, Greeks, Ottomans, travelers on the silk road, traders, and warriors have at various points in time spent the night in the Cappadocia caves.

•

It came from an explosion: the earth there is dormant lava, cut stone that holds in its belly children and in its bowels an anthill designed to thwart the ambitions of invaders. We don't know exactly how many cities there are under Cappadocia. So far thirty-seven have been found, some of which are stitched together by large, deep tunnels that fit a person riding on horseback.

•

For centuries wind and snow eroded the landscape, giving Cappadocia the appearance it has now. Since there is no place on Earth like it, Cappadocia is often compared to the moon. A single color coats the entire surface, which may be why the whole place feels unfathomable. The land is arid, awash with hills and fairy chimneys that jut from the earth in a confused procession. Because they are volcanic, the firmness of the rocks makes them vulnerable to friction: rather than build their hearths by piling stone upon stone, the men and women of Cappadocia carved their homes into the mountains. Instead of erecting large buildings, they made holes in the earth and dug out caves.

It's unlikely that any of these troglodytes were driven by the desire to have the tallest house, as often happens in other places where people flaunt their power by raising themselves as high as they can into the air. Maybe what mattered to them was for their house to be sturdier than anyone else's and deeper underground. That way the people who lived in it could tinker with the empty space and open up more room for themselves without thinning the walls, without turning the house into a rickety skeleton that would one day crash down on their heads.

•

Some rites of passage begin with a person descending into a cavern or grave: *regressus ad uterum*. There is a Turkish legend about the origin of humanity that begins in a grotto of Mount Karadağ. One of its cavities was shaped like a human silhouette. During a storm the cavern filled with water that turned to clay on contact with the earth and covered the entire anthropomorphic cavity. The sun warmed the clay figure for nine months and after those nine months had passed, the first man, Ay-Atam, rose up from there. He lived on his own for forty years, when another flood filled the cave and the earth conceived a woman. They had forty children who then went on to populate the world. When the two of them died, their firstborn buried them so they could come back to life.

•

Early Christians sought refuge in Cappadocia, fleeing martyrdom. Hence the churches and monasteries sculpted in the caves and dedicated to the worship of Jesus Christ. Perched on the mountain, the dark and windowless church of Göreme is famous for the frescoes that adorn its walls and remain well-preserved in spite of the passage of time: there, myriad fish have become trapped in all that rock.

•

Philip II of Spain, also known as Philip the Prudent, was profoundly Catholic and wanted to spread his religion to the farthest reaches of his kingdom. He liked to declare that the sun never set on his empire. Throughout history, an impressive number of sovereigns have made similar assertions and claimed to possess everything the eye could see: Genghis Khan, Alexander the Great, Charles V. Yet in Cappadocia, in the heart of Christendom, their ambitions would have met an obstacle. Cappadocia is what cannot be seen, what escapes the immediacy of the gaze.

II

We flew from Istanbul to Cappadocia and landed at dawn. Though the distance between the two cities is small, the landscape is completely different. A place at once empty and full, Cappadocia inspires bewilderment. Which is why it is useless to try and take in the landscape with only your eyes. Trees are few and far between and sunlight pours mercilessly onto your skin, drenching it. To stand in the shade or cover your head with a piece of fabric provides a singular comfort that is foreign to those of us who live in places with temperate weather. Bright red flags with a white star and crescent moon billow around us.

•

A voice I don't recognize wakes me. Before sunrise, the imam chants in Arabic at the mosque. In his throat vowels seem to find their texture and feel unending; they are sound trapped in a cave. From somewhere else in the city, another voice calls back and their words meet in the air. I know they are singing the dawn prayer, the first of five prayers that punctuate the day. I wish I could understand what they're saying. I think of the Arabic words I know: almanac, apricot, crimson, tangerine.

●

Cappadocia is the second most visited place in Turkey, after Istanbul. Travel agencies operating in what was once Constantinople advertise tours of the region with great enthusiasm, usually armed with a selection of photographs that show a panoramic view: the full expanse of tawny desert and mountains, small-windowed caves, and hot-air balloons made of bright fabrics that contrast with the pale color of the ground. Enhancing the experience is the fact that most available hotels are located inside the caves. Every day at breakfast, they serve Turkish coffee so dark and thick it is impervious to light.

●

The Göreme Open-Air Museum is one of the most popular sites in the city, located only a few kilometers from the hotels and businesses. You can rent a bike and cycle there, weather permitting. Sometimes the heat is so intense the tires will burst, and you're left with no choice but to continue on foot.

Walking over a surface covered in sand is a different experience altogether. Asphalted cities have made it impossible for us to look back at our steps, and it's easy to forget the path we took. In Cappadocia, I saw for the first time the prints my feet left on the ground as they vanished into the distance.

•

Even though Cappadocia isn't known for its camels, a Turkish man had a pair of them tied to a tree. *One lira, one photo*, he yelled. The same man had at his disposal a few items typical of Arabic dress: hijabs, a turban, necklaces. Clothes not usually worn by people in the area. Several tourists waited in line to get on the drowsy camel so they could take a photo home with them. A few steps away, in the shade of one of the hills, a patterned loveseat broke the illusion that we were in a far-off, arid land. A group of Turkish women were having an animated conversation, gesturing with their hands and roaring with laughter. I'm still not sure how different we are from those first invaders, who were unable to see the city beneath their feet.

III.

CASSANDRA

I saw nothing.
Overtaxed by the gift of sight, I was blind.
I saw only what was there,
next to nothing.

Christa Wolf

The square was coated in an ashen veil. The buildings that cordoned it and the fifty thousand square meters beneath the television tower were a single block of concrete. Whether you turned, stared at the ground, or looked ahead—it was all the same. The grayish skin covering everything left no place for the eyes to rest. A couple of kilometers away, a crowd marched from Mollstraße and gradually spilled into every corner of the square. Before noon on November 4, 1989, Alexanderplatz was packed. People from all over the country had come to take part in the largest demonstration in the history of the GDR. The somberness of the view contrasted with the euphoria of the half-million protesters.

The body of an old truck served as an ad hoc platform on which several people delivered speeches over the next three hours. Then they called her up. She wore large green glasses that made her look older, and the olive-colored pages she'd written her speech on were visible from a distance. Christa Wolf made her slow way to the platform wrapped in a dark coat. She looked up for a moment before reading, probably moved by the crowd gathered before her:

Jede revolutionäre Bewegung befreit auch die Sprache.
Every revolutionary movement also liberates language.

A few blocks from the protest, the soldiers guarding the border tried to understand what lurked beneath the commotion that had gripped Alexanderplatz. They were too busy pricking their ears to notice the wall in front of them beginning to crack or the concrete, now vulnerable to weather, slowly crumbling. Or maybe they did notice and chose to pretend that nothing out of the ordinary was happening.

Five days later, the Berlin Wall fell.

•

The buildings on this street in the Pankow district are identical. As are the various apartments. Like in a game of echoes and repetitions, the spaces are symmetrical and have similar layouts, and the same model is replicated all along this leaden block. The people who live in the building wouldn't know how to tell their homes from those of other residents if one day they returned from work to find every apartment empty, stripped of the drapes and the furniture, unable to see themselves in the objects' wear and tear.

Some residents have stuck up photographs in order to lay claim to the walls. In a first-floor apartment, a pair of girls smile in black and white at anyone who sees them. Christa Wolf's study is located at the end of the hall and her desk faces the window; had there been a garden, she would've been able to watch it change through the glass. Outside, the Cold War hardens and Christa Wolf writes *Cassandra* because she does not want history to repeat itself. She writes to avert war, even though she fears no one is listening: "I will continue a witness even if there is no longer one single human being left to demand my testimony." *Cassandra* is a warning. Wolf knew wars begin with language.

•

The priestess cursed by Apollo. Cassandra, daughter of Priam, a fallen king, eternally defeated. The god's saliva in her mouth was enough to turn her gift into a nightmare, to wrest the prophecy from her tongue. Christa Wolf embarked for the ruins of Troy in search of Cassandra. Centuries earlier—in a time of other waters and other sails—the prophetess had taken the same route in reverse, to Mycenae, knowing that there she would meet her death. A prisoner, like all the women on the defeated side, Cassandra watched the walls the gods had erected grow small as she drew away. In Troy, the walls were always first and last. "Here I end my days, helpless, and nothing, nothing I could have done or not done, willed or thought, could have led me to a different goal." Before Cassandra's eyes, Troy burned twice.

•

Cassandra first appeared as a character in the poems of Homer. Though only mentioned in a handful of verses, she stands out for her beauty, greater than any of Priam's other daughters. In Book XXIV of the *Iliad,* Cassandra notices before anyone else that her father has returned from Achilles' encampment with her brother's lifeless body on his back. This incident was enough for Euripides and Aeschylus to attribute to her the gift of divination, in return binding her to Apollo's curse, the wooden horse, and her rape by Ajax in the temple of Athena.

•

Oracles held prominent positions in ancient times. Divination was a conduit of communication between humans and gods, between the living and the dead. It was a form of religious knowledge that could be intuitive or learned. Those who wanted to become experts in the art of divination could visit temples to receive instruction from the priests on how to read the sky, augur the coming days in the movement of the stars, and scry for evidence of death in the bodies of others by rooting around the entrails of sacrificed animals.

Intuitive divination, on the other hand, was considered a divine gift. The prophesier would issue vaticinations in the sanctuary at Delphi in a state of trance, God's voice streaming from her throat and her possessed body thrashing as she heralded an inescapable fate. The character of Cassandra represents the kind of intuitive divination that refuses to trade in death.

•

It came from outside. A peculiar smell, imperceptible to the people around her, settled on the tip of her nose. The tenseness of her body and the sudden pause in her breath were the first symptoms, followed by a violent fall. Her body struck down now trembles uncontrollably, and her limbs shake as they try to unload their knowledge. Her saliva thickens to foam, a current dragging words out of her mouth. Cassandra bites her tongue to keep from speaking, from saying what needs to be kept quiet. "Who will find a voice again, and when?" She knows that she has to prevent not the incident but its pronouncement. Better to resist the revelation. The sky above Troy changes color before her eyes, its houses and temples part of a far-off dream. She can see it now. Once glorious, her city is dying out. Cassandra beholds the disappearance of everything she knows, the death of the people she loves as ever distinct. "The pain will remind us of each other. When we meet later, if there is a later, we will recognize each other by it."

•

Survivors of World War II never forgot the sight of their cities reduced to dust. "But must a man who lives when all men die be a coward?" In East Germany, the Communist dream took over from the Nazi dictatorship. A committed Marxist, Christa Wolf was convinced that you could take utopia to the people, that it could become a part of everyday life. To her, the GDR represented the possibility of a new beginning, an opportunity to rebuild Germany.

•

Time passed and the Communist dream also crumbled. The leaders of the GDR called for the construction of a wall to keep their "ideals" safe from contamination, never mind that the wall smothered some of those same ideals. They outlawed pessimism, as well as any notions or practices that might harm the unity of the State. They deemed it necessary to expel some people in order to hold many others captive. They created the Ministry of State Security, or Stasi, to surveil everything.

•

Although there were only a handful of fish markets in East Berlin, fish delivery vans were often spotted on the street. It was common knowledge that these vans carried Stasi agents who tried to mask their scent with the smell of seafood. In the GDR every citizen was watched, and anyone could be an undercover agent disguised as a paperboy, ready to jot down the brand of cigarettes purchased by their target. The spies all filed meticulous reports with painstaking detail, such as when the person ate or went to bed. A change in the subject's routine could be a sign that something was afoot. Some agents installed hidden microphones and took photographs of suspicious-looking objects. Among the Stasi's peculiarities was an obsession with hoarding paperwork. If someone were to yoke together every document like links in a chain, it would be one hundred and fifty kilometers long.

Memories of surveillance in the GDR were kept on squares of paper the size of puzzle pieces. When the wall came down, some agents did their best to destroy evidence of their investigations, but Communist austerity worked against them; the paper shredders weren't up to the task and they were forced to tear up many of the documents by hand. The people who moved into the offices of the then-defunct Stasi also inherited from them mountains of paper, scraps of photographs, and strips of photographic film.

·

The GDR ended with the Berlin Wall. As soon as there was no longer a wall dividing the country, German reunification became possible. Christa Wolf was one of several figures who strongly objected to this course of action. The prophesier could not see that the Communist dream did not exist. Maybe there's nothing more blinding than hope. "Why are we carried away by the very wishes that are grounded in error?"

•

When the two halves of Germany became one again and certain Stasi files were unsealed, Christa Wolf was criticized for her supposed collaboration with the government as a spy. "Who's guilty when everyone is guilty?" Despite the stigma that seemed to follow her, Wolf never left Germany. She lived in East Berlin until the day she died. Her work is a testament to the gradual disillusionment of society and at the same time, paradoxically, of hope.

IV.

NORMANDY

"The second thing to remember is that a real witch is always bald."

"Bald?" I said.

"Bald as a boiled egg," my grandmother said.

I was shocked. There was something indecent about a bald woman.

Roald Dahl

I

The ships landed on the beaches of Normandy before dawn. Along eighty kilometers of coastline, amphibious vessels slid out of the water like sea monsters and shook themselves dry, flinging off their damp bodies thousands of men smeared with the same euphoria of war. Insatiable, the beach seemed to devour the troops. Aircrafts helped feed the assault from the sky: one by one, the soldiers surrendered themselves to flight, to the allure of the fall. Their jellyfish silhouettes—ephemeral but perfect for slipping through the air—negotiated gravity until the feel of the sand returned to them the animal weight of their bodies.

The landings lasted more than a month and with them the war was near its end. No seaborne invasion has ever equaled that of the Allies on the coast of France. Following the tides of the English Channel, armies from all over the world gathered to free France from Nazi occupation and to contain Nazi control of Western Europe. Besides soldiers, the crew also included spies, nurses, and correspondents. Among them were Robert Capa, J.D. Salinger, and Ernest Hemingway—their eyes wide open.

•

Thanks to the work of Robert Capa, there is now a large photographic archive of the Allies' expedition in France. Many of his photographs capture in detail the textured expressions of civilians and soldiers, whose faces convey everything from the meekness of subjugation to the ecstasy of liberation, from the understanding of survival to the sheen of fear.

Among these images that bear witness to the Allies' victory over the Nazis and shed light on the jubilation that flooded the streets of French towns is a series of photographs taken in Chartres just two months after the Normandy landings. The series is a visual record of the violence deployed against women accused of carrying on relationships with German soldiers or collaborating with them. While men convicted of the same crime were killed, the women were subjected to a different kind of punishment: in a public place, as everyone watched, their hair was shorn down to their scalps. The purpose of their shaved heads was not only to provoke disgust in those who saw them but also to serve as a protracted reminder of the betrayals they were accused of.

Robert Capa's photographs manage to convey the various stages of this public shaming. The first few images capture the moment of mutilation. Some women look straight at the camera, having clearly learned to quiet their fear. The dejection on their faces is as transparent as the pleasure the men feel as they run their fingers through locks of hair that don't belong to them, demonstrating a level of intimacy exclusive to lovers and tormentors. Around them, the audience gives a satisfied smile and applauds at the hard snip of the shears.

Heads shaven, sometimes half-naked with swastikas tarred on their bodies, the women were paraded down the streets to the beat of a drum, either by foot or on top of a wagon. Their exposed scalps transformed them into abject creatures devoid of beauty. To consummate this punishment, their hair was swept into a mound that burned until the smell filled the air.

The bodies of these women had become another territory to be recaptured. Violating them was a strategy that served to denigrate the enemy and ensure the finality of defeat. The public shaming of French women turned into a widespread pursuit, a part of the everyday ritual of French liberation.

II

The practice of shaming women by shaving their heads has Biblical origins. This punishment is alluded to in several Books: Jeremiah, Isaiah, Deuteronomy, Corinthians. In each case the bald woman carries the burden of shame, and her shorn head is a stigma signifying moral weakness and vice. In Isaiah, for example, God threatens to shave off the hair of the daughters of Sion for walking with their heads held high and a suggestive gait, dressed in necklaces and jewels. In Deuteronomy, God tells his warriors that if they should come across a captive woman they find attractive and would like to marry, they must first lock her up in their houses for thirty days, stripped of the clothes of her captivity; there, she must trim her nails and shave her head. Clearly, God was banking on a loss of appeal.

•

In the middle ages, women accused of adultery had their heads shaved. In the twentieth century, the female partners of Spanish Republicans, German women who socialized with non-Aryan men, and French women who collaborated with the Germans met the same fate. Each case was a question of eroticism. What they sought to do was unsex the body that had rebelled.

•

Hair has long been viewed as a symbol of sex and status in cultures across the world. It was common among Egyptians for free people to keep their heads shaved and wear a wig. The Greeks offered hair as tribute to the gods and depicted their goddesses with long, abundant locks. There are other examples in mythology that pay special attention to hair: Delilah steals Samson's powers when she has his hair shaved; Medusa's head is covered in snakes instead of curls. The Romans were convinced that people with little or no hair were in some way deformed. During Victorian times, respectable women wore their hair up while prostitutes wore it loose.

III

My first witches were the ones in the Roald Dahl novel. It's not that I'd never seen any before. I was familiar with all of the fairy-tale witches, but none of them scared me. I always thought there was something charming and likeable about those witches. Plus, they were right to be angry.

The Dahl witches were the first ones that really frightened me, and showed me that the world could be a dangerous place. What upset me most of all was the possibility that a kind, ordinary lady could be a witch, that she could be hiding a lump of soft, toeless flesh inside her shoes, and that an innocent head scratch might in fact betray the unwelcome presence of a wig. This section gave me nightmares:

There now appeared in front of me row upon row of bald female heads, a sea of naked scalps, every one of them red and itchy-looking from being rubbed by the linings of the wigs. I simply cannot tell you how awful they were, and somehow the whole sight was made more grotesque because underneath those frightful scabby bald heads, the bodies were dressed in fashionable and rather pretty clothes. It was monstrous. It was unnatural.

A crowd of bald heads was irrefutable proof that Dahl's witches were more than just a story. The fact that the women didn't have any hair was no fantasy, and this made their recipe for turning children into mice plausible too.

•

Hair also braids my family history. My sister was six when she stopped growing. The marks my parents made on the wall to measure the passage of time remained unchanged for several months. Even though we are less than two years apart, a gulf began to open between us in those months. I behaved like I was the big sister and exercised the independence of the first-born child who can already read to herself. My sister, on the other hand, was small and quick to smile, her cheeks colored by the sun. And her hair was so long it fell down to her waist.

She was the only person who seemed not to mind the apparent sluggishness in her growth. She took advantage of all the benefits her ninety-something-centimeters afforded her for longer than was normal: she pretended to sleep so she wouldn't have to go for a walk, she never carried anything heavier than an empty lunch box, and though we never said a word about it, the bottom bunk soon became part of her domain.

The woman at the beauty salon took one look at my sister and decided she'd stopped growing because of the length of her hair; it would have to be cut. Just to the shoulder, she said as though those words made the verdict any lighter. It took just a few minutes for the sharp edge of the hairdresser's shears to trim back my sister's childhood bliss and our parents' suffocating fantasy: their daughter would grow after all, just like the other kids.

•

When my mother lost her hair, I mislaid words. Not just my own, but also words that weren't mine. Strands of my mother's brown hair wound down my throat and knotted inside me like wire. Everything I might have said was caught behind that barbed, rusted tangle. In hindsight, and thanks to the unyielding residue left by my period of quiet, I now believe that chopping my hair off might have been the only way for me to come to terms with my silence. What has stayed with me from those months is a discomfort between my ribs. A deep, stabbing pain that I feel whenever I see a woman wearing a scarf on her head.

V.

THE

OTHER

LOST BOYS

AND

GIRLS

As a time traveler, I would never be a girl more than six, not a second more . . . Barring that, I'd sit and rewrite stories written for children, which always begin: "Once upon a time . . ."

Esther Seligson

The sea slips through the breakwater without asking permission. Commanding the water and the soil it washes, the sea crashes open its jaws as a reminder of what everyone already knows: that it could swallow the island whole. The cars huddle on the far side, keeling, ashamed of their place in the world. Satisfied by this gesture, the sea retreats and lets the sweetness of rum and simmering mint warm the air and the bodies of tourists who sense that happiness might be contagious, even when it appears incomprehensible.

The narrow streets of Old Havana shield pedestrians' eyes from the tropical sun. These asymmetrical lines—only accessible by foot—are the oldest parts of the city. Here, the mixture of blood that made a home on this island has left a legacy of buildings that alternate in disarray: five centuries of accumulated desires stand on just a handful of blocks—from baroque to neoclassical, to the ruins of a wall built to ward off pirates. Ever since, Cuba has been at the threshold of two worlds: the new one, which unfolded to reveal that the border was an illusion, and the washed-out world being left behind.

Like an artery that rises out of the bay, Calle Amargura cuts through the center of Old Havana to Plaza del Cristo. Like many of the surrounding streets—Mercaderes, *merchants*; Oficios, *trades;* Cuarteles, *barracks*—Amargura, *sorrow,* takes its name from the role it played centuries ago: enslaved Africans who survived the eighty-day crossing hauled metal chains down this street before being branded by the person who had purchased them. Starting in the nineteenth century, every Friday during Lent, a Via Crucis procession would cut through the bustle from the dock to the church. In memory of the calvary, on the corner of Mercaderes and Amargura, stands a green cross that sometimes serves as a helpful landmark.

During the Cuban Revolution, the U.S. government used a printing press on Calle de Cuba to disseminate an apocryphal law that sought to ward off signs of communist sympathy and undermine budding support for Castro. According to this law, custody of Cuban children was to be transferred from the parents to the State: after being separated from their families, the children would be indoctrinated with Communist beliefs and their parents would only see them again once they were of legal age. Those with active imaginations added that the most gifted children would be sent as tribute by Castro to the Soviet Union, where they'd receive the best education available in return for serving the Revolution.

The U.S. enlisted Bryan Walsh, a Catholic priest of certain renown on the island, to help them coordinate the operation. Before the Revolution, the Church had played an influential role in Cubans' lives. Aside from being anti-Communist, the Church also had the trust of many Cuban families, which made it an excellent medium for spreading information.

Shrouded in mystery and written with precise terminology, this lie flitted through the windows of the island's families, cloaked in the factuality of the printed word. Then fear turned to dust, coating every street in the country. In October 1960, the radio announced:

> Mothers of Cuba, listen! The next law the government passes will be to take every child between the ages of five and eighteen. Mothers of Cuba, don't let the government take your children! This will be the law. When it happens, your children will become materialist monsters, and Fidel will be Cuba's supreme mother.

The Cold War hardened behind the face of a kid with baby teeth. "Operation Peter Pan," as it was dubbed by Penny Powers, an English teacher living in Cuba, would become the largest exodus of children to the United States (earlier, in other lands, the exodus had been of Jewish, Greek, and Spanish children). In the space of twenty-two months, between 1960 and 1962, more than 14,000 Cuban children were voluntarily sent to Florida. They all left Cuba on commercial flights, under the light of day. The more fortunate children traveled with their siblings, but most went unaccompanied. After all, the United States only granted visas to minors.

The air of the Havana airport grew thick with farewells instead of reunions. Children wandered with suitcases hauled behind them and waved their small hands in goodbye. Delicate trees with torn-out roots, they flew together toward an exile populated with imaginary reasons that opened up a real divide. Salt-tongued children rose above the sea. War-trophy children banished by fear. There was no one over seventeen. First went the eldest, then the kids from the richest families. Then the girls. Finally the middle-class kids and the kids between two and three years old.

•

Ana Mendieta/ arrived in Neverland with her sister Raquelín./ They were temporarily taken in by a German family,/ but got sick of doing their chores./ Cinderellas trapped in the wrong fairy tale,/ the girls asked to be sent back to the orphanage.

Ana/ became an artist/ and caked herself in mud, leaves, snow/ or camouflaged her body in tree roots./ In 1985, half-girl, half-bird,/ Ana/ fell from the/ window of the apartment she shared with Carle Andre,/ her husband,/ the only person who saw her fall/ and who told everyone she had flown out the window herself.

They lived on the thirty-fourth floor.

•

Even though Neverland has always been an island, the lost children ended up in Florida, which is no more than a spit of land. Pinned to their clothes or to pieces of fabric were signs with their names and ages written in a language that didn't belong to them. *My name is Carmen Gómez. I am five years old. Please, be good to me.* The Cuban children waited like a huddle of penguins in an airport room that was changed by their arrival: the halls had grown wider and the ceiling rose impressively over their orphaned gaze. At the end of their journey a person would read out their names, turning them into exiles.

Several camps were set up around Florida for the children. Some referred to them as "El infierno verde," the green inferno. When these turned out not to be enough, the kids were sent to any place that could house them, such as orphanages or temporary homes. It wasn't uncommon for the big kids to look after the little ones, for the children to work in the fields with nuns or in the houses where they stayed. Time stole their teeth and slowly dyed their hair another color. The country of Neverland turned out to be a fake. There were no peg-legged pirates or fairies, there was no Tiger Lily, not even a crocodile pacing around with a tick-tock in his belly.

After the Cuban Missile Crisis and their humiliating defeat at the Bay of Pigs, the United States broke off all relations with Cuba and shut down the embassy, ruining any chance the parents had of getting a visa. Some children were adopted and others, having resigned themselves to wait, were left adrift. Many Cuban parents had expected to see their children in no time at all, but this wasn't the case. We always know more about farewells than we do about reunions.

•

Boy Scout,/ said a boy with swollen eyes/ Boy Scout, said the boy a little louder./ He knew he was being called on by those/ and though he tried to answer/ his voice was caught beneath his tongue./ He shook his head./ The small boy protested:/ but Boy Scouts don't cry./ That night/ the fake Boy Scout had a dream./ The bunk bed he'd been sleeping in for months/ squashed him against the ceiling/ until there was nothing left inside.

•

Peter Pan, the character created by James Matthew Barrie, was the only boy in Neverland who never grew up. He was famous on the island for two reasons. The first was incidental: he had cut off Captain Hook's hand in a fight and fed it to a crocodile that developed a taste for the pirate's flesh. The other reason had to do with status: Peter Pan was the leader of all the lost boys who arrived in Neverland after accidentally tumbling out of their strollers and going unclaimed for seven days.

Early in Barrie's novel, Peter Pan loses his shadow in the Darling house while trying to get away. He heads back to fetch it, convinced it will be easy to patch up, that boy and shadow will come together again the moment they touch. But he's mistaken. As Peter lies disconsolate on the floor, Wendy is woken by his tears and stitches his dusky silhouette back to his feet with a needle and thread. Just like Peter Pan, a large number of Cuban children lost their shadows in strangers' houses, and no amount of mending could get their bodies to recognize them.

•

Candi Sosa/ had been singing since she was a little girl./ Fidel Castro heard her/ and was so moved he lifted her up in his arms./ Even though she dreamed of one day performing at the Tropicana,/ Candi left Cuba, just like the other kids./ Forty years after the Revolution/ Candi/ returned to the island/ with a group of Peter Pan children./ When she walked through the door of the house where she'd lived/ she took off her shoes/ so she could feel the touch of the floor on the soles of her feet.

•

Some kids were so small when they flew to Neverland that they forgot their way home and the language of their mothers. When they finally returned, they had to figure it all out again. Though at first they communicated in signs, in time they also

VI.

ÖZDAMAR'S

TONGUE

In my language, tongue means language.
The tongue does not have bones: it twists in the direction
we twist it in.
I sat tongue twisted in the city of Berlin.

Emine Sevgi Özdamar

I

She moved to West Berlin at eighteen to work in one of
the factories for six months. Eyes accustomed to the colors of
Istanbul; dark, thick hair. She wasn't one for headscarves but
in Germany the workers wore their hair in nets. She thought
of herself as a collector of words and yet knew none so far in
German. Turkish was her tongue and her mother's tongue.
She arrived in a city rent in half, arranged around a concrete
wall and its watchtowers, around control points and the efforts
of some to stop others from fleeing. Her hometown, Istanbul,
was also two cities, the border between them not stone but a
liquid line that has been there forever: the Bosporus, a strait
over which the beginning or the end of Asia and Europe gaze
at each other from either side. In its waters, the currents of
the Black Sea join those of the Sea of Marmara and together
form a single flow. South of the Bosporus, on the European
side, the sea has drawn a path in the land and split the city into
two more banks, both seven kilometers long and studded with

mosques, palaces, and the Galata Tower. In this area, known as the Golden Horn, the water is at once salty and fresh.

About the border of the city where she grew up, the city she knew best, Özdamar wrote:

> Madame Athena once told me a story about two mad-men in Istanbul: one stood on the European bank and said, "From here Istanbul is mine"; the other stood on the Asian bank and shouted across to the European side, "From here Istanbul is mine."

Perhaps Özdamar had gone to Berlin in search of another city divided by a border.

·

She arrived in 1965, when hundreds of thousands of Turks were moving to Germany. Migrants were welcome back then and no one complained about the number of foreigners cross-ing the border. They called them *Gastarbeiter*: guest workers. They arrived after the war to make up for a decimated pop-ulation that needed labor to rebuild itself. Other hands to dig mines and grow coarse in factories and in fields, other hands to sweep clean the streets and houses of dust—the ashen blan-ket that had lain over everything since the beginning of the war. Welcome only until the immaculate brilliance of the Ger-man people shone once more in the windows, and they could claim it was thanks to their willpower and to the discipline of their daily work that they were able to reinvent themselves time and again. After all, the migrants didn't speak German but *Gastarbeiterdeutsch*. The migrants didn't write in German but in *Gastarbeiterdeutsch*. The same went for their children. As though language were a thing passed down by blood.

•

Özdamar understood that stepping into another country with no return ticket meant willingly surrendering to an indeterminate foreignness, letting go in another language, and accepting that there would always be something ungraspable about words, something a little distorted that drew back whenever you thought you were getting close. But Özdamar also suspected there must be something attractive about giving up one's mother's tongue, what with all the people who were packing their lives into twenty-three-kilo bags.

•

She returned to Berlin eleven years later, fleeing a military coup in Turkey. By that point she spoke Heine's language and had studied acting in Istanbul. She went to Germany because theater was the only thing that interested her: "I get up and go to the other Berlin," she wrote. "Brecht was the first person I came here for." She lived in the West but crossed the border every day to go to Volksbühne, the theater on Rosa-Luxemburg-Platz where she assisted Benno Besson and Matthias Langhoff before staging her own plays and giving voice to Brecht's characters. Her experiences in those years inspired her to write the autobiographical novel *Seltsame Sterne starren zur Erde*, or *Strange Stars Stare at Earth*, published in 2003, part of a series titled *Sonne auf halben Weg: die Istanbul Berlin Trilogie*, or *Halfway Sun: The Istanbul-Berlin Trilogy*, which also includes *Life Is a Caravanserai* and *The Bridge of the Golden Horn*.

Strange Stars is told in two parts. It begins with a first-person account of the trips the protagonist took every day between the two halves of Berlin: books sold for a song in the East, the wall, the communes in the West filled with young people ashamed of their parents' past. The second part is a journal that features costume sketches, set designs, notes, and reflections on theater rehearsals. Most images are followed by descriptions in German; only one is in Turkish. Three men sit around a table, one of them smokes while the other two listen to him with suspicion. They wear boots, raincoats, and a hat each. They are most likely detectives or hit men. On the tablecloth is an important warning: *kırmızı*, which means red, the color of the Turkish flag.

•

In *Strange Stars*, Özdamar details her experience of migrating to and living in a new city, as well as the life she had led in Turkey and how this affected her understanding of places around Berlin. A picture of three cities emerges in a single narrative: East Berlin, West Berlin, and Istanbul.

Berlin materializes through detailed descriptions told from the perspective of a foreigner who needs time to grow accustomed to the colors and make sense of what she sees, to adapt to the world around her and learn the meanings of the words stamped all over the streets, shop windows, and train menus:

> They've all become used to me. I've become used to them. The train takes me to the theater, I get on and off, at the theater bar I buy tea for fifty pfennige, I love Mozart now; from nine to three, I rehearse, Fritz smiles at me, every day I sketch the rehearsals and get better and better at German, I read Heine.

Meanwhile, Istanbul is evoked in a haze. It exists only in memory and becomes a choice setting for nostalgia:

> It was a warm night. The lily, lit up by the car headlights, smelled pleasant. Through an open window, I heard the clinking of silverware and felt nostalgia for Istanbul. Right then, my brother, sister, and grandmother were probably on the balcony. A night in May. Outside, colorful young women were likely strolling by. When it's hot out, even the faces of Istanbul's poor grow soft.

·

Languages betray the shortcomings and inclinations of those who speak them. Germany is also a land for people with nostalgic tendencies. There are several German nouns for nostalgia. *Sehnsucht, Fernweh, Nostalgie, Wehmut, Heimweh.* This last word consists of two parts that, when combined with other words, designate particular sensations. *Weh* means pain or sorrow while *Heim* is often translated as "house" or "home." *Heim* can also be used to form other nouns such as *Heimat*, which can be translated as "home country" and refers to the relationship a person has with the place where they grew up and learned to speak, as well as with the feelings and experiences of their childhood. *Heimat* is a connection to land and language crucial to the formation of identity. A derivative of this noun exists in the adjective *unheimlich*, the negation of *Heim.* Often translated into Spanish as "siniestro" or "ominoso" and into English as "sinister" or "uncanny," *Unheimlich* speaks of a thing that breaks with the familiar and day-to-day, generating a sense of unease.

The first recorded use of *Heimweh* dates to the twelfth century, in Switzerland. The fact that the word had appeared in specialist medical texts to describe a heightened, unrelenting sadness is not surprising: *Heimweh* as sickness. *Heimweh* was exported to other German-speaking countries in the Romantic era, and until then had only ever been used in the medical field.

Agglutination is the bedrock of the German language: nouns, adjectives, and other particles are strung together to create new meaning. There are hierarchies in these constructions: the last part always designates the object referred to, while the preceding words vest it with specific qualities. In principle, *Heimweh* means "pain." But not just any pain. It is a pain felt for home, for a place that has been lost, for a language, for something we think of as ours, and which is missing.

Sometimes words and their nuances serve as thermometers. Özdamar's nostalgia is not nostalgia. It is *Heimweh*.

•

We should adopt words across languages into our everyday vernacular. Pronounce them as confidently as we do those of our childhood, mark them with our accents, voice modulations, and necessary pauses. Speak them as though they were ours, find a context for them in which their meanings explode and envelop us. Turn our mother tongues into open spaces that can accommodate any word we choose or happen to come across. Recognize others for the words they've chosen. Say "home," "body," or "ghost" in any language and assume every nuance.

•

Özdamar was awarded the Ingeborg Bachmann Prize for her book *Mother Tongue* in 1991. The German title is *Mutterzunge*, a composite word that though wrong in appearance, leaves no room for correction, and so takes on new meaning. *Mutter:* mother,

Zunge: tongue. Not as in language or idiom but as in the tongue in one's mouth, that muscular organ covered in taste buds that also articulates words. A mother's tongue, not a mother tongue, which in proper German would be *Muttersprache.* Özdamar uses this strategy of deliberate mistranslation throughout the book.

Like much of Özdamar's work, *Mutterzunge* was written entirely in German. Authors who write in languages that are not their own are frequently interrogated about their motivations, as though words were also private property. Perhaps hidden behind this line of questioning lies a suspicion of betrayal or assault, an aversion to things illegitimate in appearance that can only be expressed through relentless probing. Perhaps people believe deep down that authors who do not write in the language of their mothers are taking something that is not theirs, that they are writing where they don't belong, that they are word thieves. Especially when they write in the kind of language in which a single term can refer to something that is foreign and strange, something that is unknown and that belongs to another: *Fremdsprache*, a foreign language but also the language of another.

Emine Özdamar was no doubt also hounded by this question. Before I came across her answer, I had assumed Özdamar wrote in German as a way to lay claim to the country she'd chosen to live in and, at the same time, to assert her identity as a migrant and as a Turkish woman by choosing the words that would define her, by taking up her pen and fashioning herself against the gaze of others.

Writing in German in order to say:

I [and lay claim to the blank space that complements every clause].

Instead of reading or hearing:

She [and always feeling other in relation to a multitude of words that by virtue of repeated use are in danger of prevailing, becoming real].

I came across one response in *Strange Stars*:

> I am unhappy in my language. For years, we've only spoken sentences like: "They'll hang them," "Where are their heads?" "No one knows where their graves are," "The police have not released the bodies!" Our words are sick. My words are in need of a sanatorium, like sick mussels. There is a place in the Aegean Sea where three sea currents come together. People take sacks of mussels there from Istanbul, Izmir, and Italy, where they've gotten sick in the filthy water. The clean water from these three currents heals the sick mussels in a matter of months. Fishermen call this part of the sea the mussel sanatorium. How long does it take a word to heal? They say people lose their mother tongues in foreign countries. But can't this happen too in a person's home country?

Foreign words have no childhood, wrote Özdamar. Which means their roots are not as deep and their branches are brittle.

How can a person reject their mother tongue without also rejecting their childhood? Özdamar writes in German as a way to ward off unhappiness and reject violence. Running away might also be a kind of word sanatorium. "I remember now phrases my mother spoke in her mother tongue, but only then, when I imagine her voice, do her words reach my ears, like a foreign language that has been learned well."

Özdamar posits another answer to this question in another piece: "In German, I became happy again; maybe this is why I write in it."

II

I was twenty-two when I received a scholarship to study German one summer at a university in Erfurt, a small city in eastern Germany with a population of just over 200,000, known only for the mustard it produces. The medieval quarter and castle give it the appearance of another time.

I met a couple of Turkish women in Erfurt who traveled with me to Berlin once the German course had ended. They were called Büşra and Gülcan, and I never figured out the right way to pronounce their names. We rode the train to the largest train station in Europe, Berlin Hauptbahnhof, a glass and steel shell that's five stories tall,where over a thousand trains and three hundred thousand people cross paths every day. The station pulses near where the wall once stood, and is the new gateway between East and West. Its structure has the shape of an exoskeleton. The Berlin Hauptbahnhof is a new Tower of Babel, where arrows and silhouettes framed in dichromatic squares are symbols of a language that claims to be universal.

In my mind, Berlin began as a gridded map that I carried in my backpack and studied regularly whenever I went out. Because I'm right-handed, east lies next to my pinkie finger on my map. An imaginary line draws an easy path between the Charlottenburg Palace and the television tower in Alexanderplatz. Even though I could understand the signs on the street corners, it still took me longer than usual to get my bearings. I've always envied anyone who understands where north and south are. The paper map seemed to show a different, simpler city. These days I know that the best way to find your way around Berlin is to walk, because body and mind learn out of step.

There are Turkish people all over Berlin, and it wasn't hard to find someone to give Büşra and Gülcan directions to the place where we'd be spending the night. Ramadan had started a week earlier, and I had fasted with them for a couple of days. The first time I went around Berlin was on an empty stomach. Maybe that was why I was so impressed by it.

Our first night there we had dinner in Kreuzberg, a neighborhood in Berlin also known as Little Istanbul, where people speak Turkish on the streets and drink black tea around the clock, and where the shops smell of baklava honey. During Ramadan, the fast is broken at dinner with dates and tea. I don't think anything sweeter has ever melted in my mouth.

Though I've forgotten what language my Turkish friends and I spoke together, I remember clearly the first time I saw them unveiled. In memory, words become frail and unstable, they adapt to the places we take them to and are distorted by distance. It's other things that stay with us. Maybe we spoke *Denglisch*, an improvised mix of English and German common among foreigners in transit. An improvised language that exists outside grammar and has no correct accent or clear-cut spelling, a language that is there to be spoken, and for us to quickly forget what was said in it.

I've since returned to Berlin without the tongues of Büşra and Gülcan to translate what other Turkish men and women say on the streets, as well as the restaurant menus and hand gestures. It's a different city.

VII.

KOBLENZ

Your first thought upon awakening be: "Atom." For you should not begin your day with the illusion that what surrounds you is a stable world.

Günther Anders,
"Commandments in the Atomic Age"
Frankfurter Allgemeine Zeitung
July 13, 1957

The police knocked on doors. They swept every block in an 1,800-meter radius. They instructed the residents of every house to draw the curtains and open the windows. Glass is the first thing to break. Then they should pack essentials: passports, important paperwork, enough clothes to last them a few days. The city was being evacuated as a matter of urgency. The hospitals and the train station, the prison and the hotels; no one could stay, no one could come back until further notice. It took one word for the streets to be deserted. The warning sounded like an echo that turned everything brittle: roofs, routines, appearances. It was Sunday morning and the city was, unexpectedly, fragile.

•

The deserted city is reflected on the watery surface of the Rhine. Koblenz had risen on its shores. The word Rhine comes from the Celtic word for "flow": first came the Teutons, then the French who fled the revolution, then the wars that reduced the city to rubble. The last war ended seventy years earlier, and every threat evokes a past gathering dust in museums. People walk the streets with sure steps, as though wanting to fill the space they occupy with their certainty, but it works the other way around; it's the city that gives people confidence. Koblenz asserts its permanence everywhere—in the red and green traffic lights that govern the flow of the streets, in the bus schedule, and in the ink on the newspaper.

The rain stopped and the Rhine waned. The drop in the water level was so steep that the river let go of a secret it had kept hidden in its arms: jutting from the surface was a historic splinter that had for decades lain under the mineral bottom. It showed up right when relief seemed possible. Like gauze left under the patient's skin during a surgical procedure, causing infection after the body is stitched up, so was the Rhine bomb anchored to the water's essence. A bomb that had left no sign and that the water had made invisible. No one had seen it, so nobody feared it. Under everyone's gaze, the bomb turned into a bomb again. By naming it, they invoked fear. Which is why people left their houses so quickly. Koblenz has been evacuated four times since the end of the war. This time it took 45,000 people a single morning to flee the city.

•

In the center of the radius sleeps a bomb lulled by dreams of gunpowder and ash. An age-old, rusted shell that weighs 1.8 tons. If detonated by accident, the explosive material inside it could raze every tree, house, and building for an entire block. The blast would reach even farther, stealing down streets and through windows in the second after the explosion and splintering everything in its path, like a malignant tide ejected by the waters of the Rhine.

For every ten bombs the Allies dropped on enemy territory, there are two that didn't explode. Merged with the rubble, they now sustain cities and are hidden underneath museums and monuments, beneath soccer stadiums and schools. Dormant bombs regularly show up on reconstruction sites or tangled in fishing nets. Deactivating them has become a routine procedure for German bomb disposal technicians who handle thirty or so tons of grenades and other explosives every year. Experts believe that there are still at least 3,000 bombs underneath Berlin. The city would be hollowed out into a crater if they all went off at the same time. The Ruhr Valley, Hamburg, Cologne, and Berlin are the most populous areas of Germany. The largest number of bombs is hidden in precisely these regions.

In Latin, *bombus* means noise. So a bomb is its blast, the thunderclap of things falling to pieces. If there was a word for a bomb that has not exploded, it would have to allude to silence and also to the tension produced by the chance that this silence might break from one moment to the next.

•

A metallic arm scraped at the ground in Bonn. It rose a few meters, then rested over the area and dug in a single claw that came out covered in earth. A tedious operation for the man behind the wheel of the excavator. The machine's gears creaked more than usual in the January cold. Beneath the earth, by accident, metal met with metal. The bombs stirred from their slumber with a bang. A cloud of dust rose up from the ground, and the only thing anyone around could know for sure was that the smell of gunpowder had mixed with the smell of diesel burned off by the excavator. How do we count the growing number of the dead and wounded in a war that has already ended? Maybe every instance of the past exploding beneath our feet will end up on a list of workplace accidents.

•

Every bomb bears the name of its place of origin. It's easy for bomb disposal technicians to know how far they have traveled, who made them, and where. The more they know about the bomb, the easier it is to defuse it, to guess what's inside and forecast its range. But a bomb that protrudes from the ground is always dangerous. The slightest vibration can activate the chemical substances that reside within it. As soon as a bomb becomes visible, it is liable to explode at any point in the next five days. Sometimes the only thing explosive experts can do is draw a radius of safety and evacuate the area inside it. The explosion of these bombs is the echo of the ones that came before it, the grinding of memory. The destruction they produce defies all anachronism: they're bombs dropped by soldiers who are long dead and yet continue to cause destruction.

•

After he was awarded the Nobel Prize for Literature, Elias Canetti refused to grant another interview. He stopped traveling and lived a quiet life between London and Zurich. He'd fled war since he was a child, and moved all around Europe. A diligent student of the languages spoken in every city he lived in, he dedicated the same careful attention to the air raids that wrecked them. He had a very long life, long enough to witness nearly every twentieth-century war. He spent thirty-five years writing his masterpiece, *Crowds and Power*, in which he analyzed, in the shadow of war extermination, the way that crowds function and how they are controlled.

Fifteen meters below ground, in a bunker of the Zentralbibliothek Zürich, lies Elias Canetti's legacy: a private library of fifteen thousand books, and one hundred and four boxes of notes, journals, and correspondence. Per the author's wishes, no one is to be given access to the material until 2024, by which time all of the people referenced in his notes will have most likely died. Canetti's words will continue to speak of war, crowds, and extermination; they will not have expired. They too will explode, and they will be like splinters to the people who hear them.

•

For the residents of Koblenz, leaving the city must have been like catching a glimpse of the past. Much like the impression left by old photographs of relatives we don't know, strangers in whose faces we recognize certain traits. Maybe the people of Koblenz saw in the empty streets and in their forced getaway a sliver of the city's history. A history inescapably bound with their own.

Though Natalia Ginzburg survived the war, it stayed with her for the rest of her life. The sound of bombs exploding rang in her ears and followed her everywhere she went. In one of her essays, she touches on the same uncertainty that gripped Koblenz:

There has been a war and people have seen so many houses reduced to rubble that they no longer feel safe in their own which once seemed so quiet and secure. This is something that is incurable and will never be cured no matter how many years go by. True, we have a lamp on the table again, and a little vase of flowers, and pictures of our loved ones, but we can no longer trust any of these things because once, suddenly, we had to leave them behind, or because we have searched through the rubble for them in vain.

•

When the residents returned to Koblenz, they were probably relieved to find their books and shoes exactly where they had left them. Not even a fine film of dust attested to their absence. At home, people were comforted by the furniture and by the grass, which had grown longer in the garden. Maybe someone noticed the particular light that objects and people emanate when they reveal their ephemeral nature. But there's no record of this. The vestiges left by bombs, even when they don't explode, tend to subsume everything. For a few days, no articles were published about any of the bombs found in other cities. Also absent from the news—in an appeal to common decency—were the millions of Euros made every year by arms dealers in Germany. No one wrote a word about it. Yet the headlines of every newspaper in Koblenz made note of the bomb that was found at the bottom of the Rhine. The articles recounted every logistical step taken to evacuate the city and highlighted the formidable training of the artillerymen who defused it. They took the bomb to a safe place in the outskirts of the city, where it exploded and no one was able to hear. Its blast was a silent cry, impossible to remember.

VIII.

BERLIN

A crack ran through Berlin.
And since a crack can't exist on its own
they built a wall to contain it.
It was the crack, not the wall, that showed.

Fabio Morábito

After the war, Berlin was a sheet of rubble. The city was rebuilt out of the ruins. People go there in search of something that no longer exists, which is why they disapprove of the younger buildings and of the freshly painted streets. The newer parts bother them because they look fake. Berlin opens its arms to people who have become sick of the world and want to visit wastelands, unlived-in houses, and empty museums, people content with documents that attest to the fact that something once stood there. In Berlin, the past is a dense fog that refuses to lift. The city stands out because it trades in reversal: the echo is sharper than the sound, memory is stronger than the present, and in public you are only allowed to conjugate in the past tense.

It's a perfect city for map aficionados. At least three different maps are needed to make sure you don't get lost: the one with rings like a seashell's for the public transit system, the one that tracks the invisible wall and pinpoints the locations of museums and monuments, and finally an ordinary map with the names of streets and cross streets. It's not uncommon for people who haven't been in Berlin very long to feel at odds with the language of these impossible-to-collate maps: the city requires you to think in sections. It can be tricky to find your way around Berlin because the city has no center but rather several centers, and the wall that once lined the city is only helpful to those who had the chance to get used to it. A Berliner will say "that's where the wall used to be," as they point at the border with their index finger and stretch out their arm to show distance.

•

In East Berlin, the wall unified a single desire and planted the same thought in everybody's minds: to cross over to the West. The first person to succeed was the soldier Konrad Schumann, whose job it was to patrol the border. That jump—just an impulse, the body folding briefly above the concertina wire— became famous in just a few days thanks to a photograph memorializing the event. Tightrope walkers, speculators, and a couple of reporters knew that Konrad Schumann's feat marked the beginning of an era of escapes and desertions.

Inspired by Schumann, a number of Germans became pioneers in the art of escape, and their competitive nature made sure that they always had a substantial advantage over other dissident groups. Still, these fugitives would never have been able to perfect their getaway techniques without help from the Stasi, which kept a meticulous record of every attempted escape and was constantly adding new obstacles to the border.

•

The first people to pass through the wall were not the ones who crossed it, but those who tried to imagine what was on the other side. In West Berlin, the wall was a canvas on which residents cast their fantasies about the city and the people on the other side; they disregarded the dryness of the wall and covered its skin in the faces, words, and colors of their imagined city. After they ran out of room to paint and escape stories no longer seemed so exciting, they built viewing platforms so they could poke their heads over. But only the tourists used it. West Berliners preferred to stick to the illustrations on the wall.

•

Despite its modest size, the Checkpoint Charlie Museum is one of the most popular museums in Berlin. On view is an exhibit of the various attempts made to cross the wall, as well as some of the artifacts used: the gas tank of a car that could fit a woman inside, a flying device, scraps of fabric from a hot-air balloon, a harness and shovels used to dig tunnels. Outside the museum, men dressed as soldiers speak English in German accents and take pictures with tourists. For a Euro, they will stamp your passport with a temporary entry visa for a country that no longer exists.

•

I only made sense of how Germany had been divided after I saw it on a map. The country's distribution cannot be understood from the perspective of symmetry or with reference to cardinal points. Even though there was an East and a West, all of Berlin was embedded on the oriental side. Berlin was an island surrounded by land, a country within a country.

Because the wall was the gateway between the two cities, many East Berliners were tricked. There were taught to believe that the wall had been built to staunch the flow of runaways that threatened to leave the cities empty, when its real purpose was to create a visual border, to confine the gaze. A wall is a collective blindfold that shields people from shame, the physical manifestation of a recurring human fantasy: to live where no one can see us.

You can only call a wall a wall when it is taller than the people looking at it and forces them to raise their heads, even if it makes no difference. A wall always appears larger when looked at head-on, and its dry skin smarts. To cross the wall and render it inoffensive you have to take several steps back, until it's just another line on the horizon. Much like fear, the size of a wall is a question of distance.

•

For twenty-eight years, East Germany and West Germany were Siamese twins joined at the spine with a common heart: Berlin, a city with a large, flaky scab forty-three kilometers long. One day the wall will be a scar, but before that it was a fence made of barbed wire.

•

The differences between the residents of East Berlin and West Berlin hardened into slabs of concrete and wire fences from one day to the next. Even though a consensus was reached about the official date of Germany's division—August 13, 1961—no one knows for sure when the wall's construction began. There are those who think it all started when a man walking down Sonnenallee reached out his arms and called one side East and the other West. Some think it was when Walter Ulbricht mentioned in an interview that no one in the East had any intention of building a wall. Others contend it was the fault of the women who shoveled up what had been left of the city after the war, because the debris they collected later went on to become the concrete that would eventually go by the name "wall." The most discerning among them allege that the real culprit was Oscar Wilde, who sowed separatist feeling in his story about the giant who builds a wall around his garden so that he won't have to share it.

•

When the end of the wall was pronounced on November 9, 1989, East Berlin was pure cheer. The section that separated the two sides shook under everyone's steps. Wall jumpers came together and spilled over the old border, crossing it again and again just for the pleasure of seeing the tracks they left on the ground. The temptation to cross soon disappeared. The border had opened, and suddenly there was nowhere to run.

The people of Berlin tore down practically the whole wall. Some did not give in to the euphoria and held on to their piece. They wanted a souvenir of the impulse to flee, of the impetus for desertion that had once filled the city.

Even though the wall has been gone for over twenty-five years, there are still two Berlins. It is believed that after German reunification, the West came out on top. After all, the name they had given the city and their version of the story ultimately prevailed. But people travel to Berlin in search of the crack, the imaginary line that haunts the city.

IX.

MIMESIS

IN

VHS

I

In the apartment where we grew up, the only things my sister and I cared about were the sofa, the VCR, and the twenty-nine inches of gray, convex screen that for years played back the stories that defined our every day. We had a tower of movies that grew in size month after month, a large structure crammed full of black boxes and plastic bricks that, instead of a skeleton, had two reels connected by a single arm: a strip of tape half an inch wide that was rewound again and again in ninety-minute intervals. We started with that tower and then saw everything.

We watched the movies so often they aged. Spots covered the television screen and certain frames lost the seamlessness and clarity of sound that had once brought them to life. In return, our laughter was stamped all over the tape, and melded with it. The worn images are still there, proof that shared happiness is a place you can go back to.

•

I look up the word for VCR—"videocasetera." It's gone. Maybe this explains why time seems to shrink when I write it down or say it aloud. The body is extinct, and the word that gives it meaning has begun to melt away, making room for others probably headed toward a similar fate. I fear that the passing of this word—like many before it—will unleash a wave of forgetting, that its evanescence will sweep away everything around it—as with the machine in *Eternal Sunshine of the Spotless Mind* that purges the mind of painful memories. Our memories are likely more fragile than I'd thought, a knot from which one thing cannot be unloosed without the rest of it coming undone.

How am I meant to talk about all the hours that were filtered through that retired object with people who've never seen one? I could call up its shape on the table, outline its exact perimeter with my fingers, sketch the rectangle of the machine's mouth, draw out the whole length of the dusty cable. Though maybe if people saw my old VCR in action they'd feel disappointed, and maybe the experience is more attractive in the imagination than it is in practice—much like a months-long boat trip, or the body's weightlessness as it rises in the basket of a hot-air balloon.

•

My sister and I had a game we used to play. We'd take turns sending each other a phrase of no fewer than five words and no more than ten, at a random point in the day. The other person would have to guess what movie it came from: *Nobody messes with a dwarf in a red raincoat / You've thrown off the emperor's groove / This'll make a new bug out of ya.*

The contest was supposed to jog our memory, which would immediately reel through hours of tape. First it would dive into the usual references: movies we were embarrassed to admit that we liked, everything Meryl Streep, movies with predictable endings, movies we hated every second of, movies that still made us laugh when we thought about them. Then it delved into more obscure places: movies we'd turned off halfway through out of boredom or because we were tired, the ones we didn't get to watch in the movie theater, the movies we each watched on our own.

There was no deadline for coming up with an answer. We could spend weeks searching for the place the phrase had been clipped from in order to patch it back together, but if we took too long a nagging feeling would begin to settle in—like an itch that won't let up. I don't remember when we last played, or which one of us was the last person to have an orphaned sentence floating around her head. But I know for certain that our relationship is woven from the meters and meters of magnetic tape that we watched together.

II

Months ago I was waiting outside a playground. The entrance had been designed to resemble a border—as fictional as any border—and visitors were welcomed by a miniature airplane cockpit. In front of me, a line moved very slowly, soft like a caterpillar trying to shake off the sun. Its larva-like body pressed in the direction of a fake airline desk where children and grown-ups paid for a bracelet that granted them entry to a city built to scale. There, the landscape and setting had shrunk.

Discouraged, I decided to observe the people in the crowd: some leafed through newspapers, others checked their watches or looked down at their phones. Near me stood four or five girls who also waited, probably more frustrated than I was, since time passed before their eyes at a viscous speed. I hadn't been paying much attention to them before they started screaming, but the sounds they made weren't natural; there was no fear or emotion in the background, just an exaggerated signal of distress that became an awkward squawking that abused their throats.

The sound in question was a greeting. The girl they were waiting for to enter the park had finally arrived. As soon as she saw her playmates, she picked up her pace and tried to make up for the delay by screeching in a similar manner. The girls hugged as though they hadn't seen one another in months or had recently survived an earthquake. One of them moved in a way that suggested weeping, bringing her hand to her mouth.

The spectacle I'd witnessed had left me grouchy and I decided to wait somewhere else, even though I knew the girls' gestures and childish choreographies were learned behaviors. I know that these girls had seen them repeated over and over onscreen for at least a decade of their lives. I also know that their squawking was the emotional simulation they were most familiar with.

·

I thought about those girls as I watched people react to the two missionaries with Ebola who landed in Atlanta. It was cinematic: the doctors lowered the patients off the plane; swaddled in white outfits, their bodies were belted to the stretchers and their faces hidden behind masks that resembled helmets. Dozens of photographs were taken in the span of several minutes and for a brief moment those images became the most important piece of news in the United States. The missionaries were transferred to a hospital where a small, riotous crowd armed with chants and posters called for them to be thrown out of the country. The reporters' cameras and photographs inflamed the group of protestors, who had by then positioned themselves with the hospital as their backdrop.

I don't believe there's a difference between a group of ten-year-old girls simulating emotion outside a playground under a toy plane and the protestors in Atlanta performing fear, aware of all the thousands of eyes watching them. Not just any eyes, but eyes that multiplied at an uncontrollable rate.

•

I can't stop reading news articles about Ebola: a woman has been self-isolating in Berlin for days because the doctors suspect she's been infected; a Spanish priest has died even though he was given the experimental drug ZMapp; the myths that people in affected regions surround themselves with is not helping them fight the virus. As I scroll through the photos I can't help but think of all the movies I've watched about pandemics and contagions. The same words are often used in both: experimental, emergency, spread, crisis, panic, vaccine, control. The lesson in these tapes is simple but true: fear is more contagious and lethal than any virus or bacteria.

•

Several photographs of the Ebola virus have been published. Perhaps as proof that it exists. It resembles a red earthworm tangled around its own body, floating in a saline solution.

•

I wonder to what extent people's reactions and the stories reported are shaped by the fact that the epicenter of the virus is in Africa, the Black continent, the home of HIV and guerrilla warfare, the perfect setting to feed our cinematic imagination, to situate otherness.. The news is just another simulation, releasing pieces of information that satisfy the morbid curiosity of people who insist on looking at others to convince themselves that their way of life is more valid than anyone else's. Their columns and headlines insist on reminding us that in Africa people protect themselves against the virus with ineffective methods that don't require needles or gloves: saltwater, raw onions, coffee beans. They also insist on highlighting other extreme measures: in Monrovia, the capital of Liberia, armed men had stormed a hospital, where they broke down doors and burned sheets covered in blood while screaming that that place, their neighborhood, was free of Ebola. Most of the patients in the hospital fled after the attack.

•

British Airways, Arik Air, and Asky Airlines are not the only companies that have suspended flights to Guinea, Sierra Leone, and Liberia; the most important Middle Eastern airline has also canceled all travel to and from the region. As a consequence of this refusal, airports have begun to empty out. This time clear skies do not spell quiet. What they mean is that the rest of the world has deemed this piece of sky and this strip of land undesirable until further notice. The day is August 11, 2014.

III

I head back to the living room of my apartment, the 5x4-meter rectangle where I also learned to contemplate fear. I've never enjoyed disaster or pandemic movies. They fill me with dread and don't produce even a bit of pleasure. I'm not partial to war movies either. But if I'm drawn to the cinematography or the story, I'll take a dose of anxiety for the sake of the gratification, which tends to outlast the tape. Maybe it's the same for the residents of Atlanta, who recognize that their city has become a stage, that they are the characters. This limelight, which is equal parts terrifying and pleasurable, is also irresistible.

X.

TRÜMMERFRAUEN

It is time the stone made an effort to flower

Paul Celan

Brick storage site on Möckernstraße in Berlin
(Ziegelstein-Lager in der Berliner Möckernstraße).
Photograph by Gerhard Gronefeld, December 1945.

The photo isn't as old as it looks. It's the first winter following the end of a war that feels as though it took place a long time ago, now that so many of the people who experienced if first-hand aren't around to call it by its name. The only edges over which the light gradates are black and white, and the absence of color tricks the eyes, opening a chasm between the image and the person observing it. There are no shadows. From its zenith the sun commands one half of the day, though we don't know if it has just begun or if the workers are about to go home; their bodies, eyelids, and hunger are what set the rhythm.

In wintertime daylight is fleeting. They'd better hurry.

•

In German, the noun *Trümmer* means debris or ruins. The Austrian and German women who rebuilt their cities using the vestiges of war were called *Trümmerfrauen*. Whether in Berlin or Hamburg, in Dresden or Vienna, they all did the same job: picking up rocks, sweeping up dust, picking up rocks, sorting them. There is no masculine form for *Trümmerfrauen*. The reason for this is obvious. By the end of 1945 there were seven million more women than men in Germany. Most of them widows or orphans.

•

Maybe, thinking they were good at sewing, good at darning and mending what was broken, the Allies assumed they could do the same for the scraps of cities and houses. Though most of the women worked in the postwar cleanup in return for a bowl of soup or a piece of bread, some were volunteers. Maybe they rummaged through the rocks on a personal quest, or maybe they just needed to talk. Sometimes words hide themselves too, and you have to dig them out to find them.

The *Trümmerfrauen* worked with paleontological precision, and always in groups because some jobs should not be done alone. They turned over the wreckage with picks and shovels in search of bricks and other materials that could be repurposed for new constructions. The bricks traveled from chaos to harmony in very long lines: from hand to hand and fallen buildings to city warehouses, where they were cut before being stored.

Maybe, before finding a suitable piece, the women would cast their eyes over the deformed arsenal of rubble and recognize rocks or objects that had once formed a part of their homes, their schools, or the churches they attended on weekends. Maybe they found among the remains something that looked familiar—a shoe or a smell—but ignored it, sensing that the thing itself would hold no meaning outside the place where it belonged.

The photographer who watched the women from a distance probably guessed that the skin of the hands that held his camera was different from the skin of these women, which became more and more like the rocks they guarded. He knew that the *Trümmerfrauen* had no age and that they were all over the country, cleaning streets and rooting through the debris.

·

Even though it seems like the bricks that crowd the image would somehow encompass every brick in the country, no camera could have captured the four hundred million cubic meters of ruins that had to be removed from the streets of Germany. The scene in front of us is only a sliver of the work that went into reconstruction: the storage site on Möckernstraße in Berlin, where the bricks salvaged from foundations and dismembered buildings were sorted before being reintegrated into the geometry of the city. Berlin became a parenthesis filled with rocks: one third of the city was razed by air raids and half the residential buildings lay unusable underground.

The stillness is evidence of the end of the war. The *Trümmerfrauen* work in silence. Their just-thick-enough clothes protect them from the glassy cold of northern Germany. An older woman selects each brick and tends to its imperfections; as she cleans it, she also cleanses her memories. Submerged in a mountain of rocks that does not crush her but instead seems to hold her up, the woman moves slowly, as if at sea, as if it was the water and not the rocks that cradled her.

At the center of the photograph is another woman who walks down a path lined by wood tracks that distribute work throughout the city. Stoically, she hauls the rocks. She draws them into her arms as though they were hers. The woman is patient as she places them one by one in the stacks earmarked for reuse; they are all the same shape.

On the far right is a woman's black silhouette. Maybe she knows she's being watched and has decided to turn her back and count the bricks she has left until she's earned a break. The pair of trees that rise through the middle of the image are just as bound to the earth as these women; they too could live nowhere else. Their roots, locked in the ground, hold the promise of foliage that will one day again cast shade.

The desire to rebuild a place is no different from the urge to never leave it, regardless of how much it has changed. After the war, most women found it impossible to leave their cities. Maybe they believed the rocks still held the scent of the people.

•

Sorting rocks was the only way to sort through language so that it could be used to name a drastically changed world. Like a brick, every word had to be examined before it was added to a new construction, before a decision was reached about the ones that would be placed above the rest and the ones that would no longer be used. The double S [ss] used in the spelling of certain words was replaced with an Eszett [ß], so that *Strasse* became *Straße*, and every street name in the country was changed to avoid any painful associations.

Nothing better illustrates the German language than this mountain of rocks anxious for order, destined to hold up buildings meant to be lived in or contemplated. German words are like rocks pieced together, one to the other and then to the other until meaning—sometimes visual, sometimes metaphorical—is formed: *Wort* means "word" and *Schatz* means "treasure" and together—*Wortschatz*—they translate into "vocabulary." *Stern* is "star," *Bild* is "painting" or "image," and *Sternbild* is "constellation." But the same word when added to another can also trigger an entirely different meaning: *Ziegelstein-Lager*, which refers to the brick storage site that Gronefeld shot in 1945, has nothing to do with the word *Konzentrationslager*: concentration camp.

·

Möckernstraße was once at the heart of Berlin's reconstruction. The street is wide and straight, much like every other street. Each angle follows the city's elaborate postwar designs. On either sidewalk, the shade cast by perfect rows of unbelievably green trees embraces passersby and bicycles in a constant rush. It's a nice street to live on and to wander down.

Not very far from here, no more than two kilometers east, stands a monument erected in memory of the *Trümmerfrauen*: a woman made of stone and surrounded by bricks glances around with empty, porous eyes and an expressionless face. In her right hand is a mallet that rests against the fabric of her skirt. The woman rests, in the middle of a forgotten park in Berlin.

XI.

BLUEPRINT

FOR A

HOUSE

We have to learn to name the places objects occupy in space. This is one reason the description of rooms and streets is such a common beginner's exercise for anyone learning a foreign language. Usually the goal is to write the blueprint of the place where we live. The house being the quintessential location. Logic would lead us to believe that the bed we sleep in and the walls we see every day should be easy to describe since we have no trouble calling them to mind, but this a false assumption: houses are stitched to our bodies, they live within us.

The end goal of these exercises is to learn how to use prepositions, to weave together words in such a way that one becomes dependent on the other. This grammatical tension washes into the bedroom and orders everything inside it: under an armchair, in front of the window, and the diagonal light that spills over the desk. The objects arrange themselves in singular harmony and sustain everything around them. A bedroom is also a collection of statements.

German prepositions vary depending on the movement or stillness of the thing referred to. Declensions are predicated on this divide. A bird that flies over a bridge is not the same as a bird that perches on it. Though there are more prepositions in Spanish, the structure of the language contains no such nuance. Describing a space in German implies contemplating it in circulation. Picturing it in terms of the motion it holds, as though it were a photograph on which the course of each journey has been marked and where the color betrays diluted forms.

Do things move or do they stay still? I ask my students whenever I teach them this subject. They need to learn to allow for change, variation, and displacement. I always ask them to describe their bedroom or their house. There are some who do so as though looking down through the roof, like a little girl peeking into a doll house with a pair of intrusive, brown eyes. And there are those who note the color of the furniture or mention the mess of books on their desk or on the nightstand by their bed.

We should only call home spaces we can fumble through in the dark.

·

The rules for sketching the blueprints for a house are precise. Like a cartographic chart, they should show an aerial view. When drawing a blueprint you need to bear in mind that each line is representative: one centimeter equals one meter (1:100), though it can also equal other measurements, since there are about as many scales as there are ways to arrange the statements that make up a house.

In a blueprint, the lines around the edges tend to be darker because exterior walls are usually somewhere between twenty and thirty centimeters thick while interior walls are between ten and fifteen. Doors are always depicted as open, with a fan-like shape marking the path they would draw on the floor. When it comes to windows, the line will need to be interrupted.

The same logic applies to writing a house.

Façade 1:150

We live *in* number 7. Our house is part *of* a series of twenty-six cookie-cutter houses. They were all designed and built in the same year. They have the same finish and the same white walls and wood floors. Some are identical in layout and space, while others are mirror images of the house next door: a young couple lives in house number 6, and we've been able to hear their son *since* the day he was born; he's learning to talk now. House number 8 belongs to the Kurtzes. He is German and she is from northern Mexico; they spend most of their time in the U.S. and only come here *during* the holidays. The houses match *on* the outside too, the same pale colors and warm roof tiles, identical height—the differences are in the details. Which is why our neighbors rushed to add plants and bicycles *to* the front of their houses. They needed a way to show which one of the twenty-six was theirs.

Living Room 1:125

The wood door begins at the ceiling and ends at the tips of our toes. It's tall, as though guarding the house of a giant. The door sits in a discreet frame whose wood grain is hidden *beneath* a coat of dark paint. The door opens and the stillness of the white house unfolds *before* our eyes. The first thing that jumps out is the braided rug in the middle of the living room, an orange rectangular surface and the best place to rest after a long day. There, before dinner, we stare *up* at the ceiling and tell each other what we got up to outside the house, the nuances of our routine, the passing inclement weather. On the orange area rug we sort through words that are not ours.

Entryway 1:100

We could measure how close we are to the people who visit our house *according to* what they do *with* their shoes when they come indoors. Our friends take their shoes off straightaway while saying hello and filling us in on the traffic. It's been a long time since we've felt embarrassed about asking them to do it, and we no longer have to offer them the sandals we reserve for guests, since they know where to find them and which ones are most comfortable. Some weekends they come over to play dominos; we drink wine and the evening whizzes by. There is the sound of music, laughter, and the clicking of pieces noisily shuffled *around* the table. More than once during a match I have found myself glancing up and past the domino set to my friends' shoes lined up *beside* ours at the back of the living room. I look back down at my pieces and think of how lucky I am.

Study 1:75

On the first floor, the light comes in *from* the side of the house. This is the space we've set aside for work. Our desks—one white and the other brown—are separated by a loveseat that's meant for reading. In the study we can't look at each other head-on; we can only hear each other. I like listening to the sound of typing as the house fills with the drive behind those long fingers. It's nice when an arrhythmic noise begins to feel comforting. Learning to write in company means getting used to sharing an unavoidable series of smudges and cross-outs.

Balcony 1:50

There are days when the walls feel too white. Now and then I think it might be nice to live in another house, but all I have to do is follow that train of thought for it to start to seem ridiculous: I picture moving, the books packed into numbered boxes, the furniture covered in plastic, and the process of slowly getting used to sleeping in a new room. It'd be a foolish thing to do, since if I lived in another house I'd want it to be just like this one.

Backyard 1:25

There's a picture window *between* the dining area and the backyard. We stuck a vinyl sticker on the glass in the shape of cherry blossoms that hang off a couple of branches. For a while the garden was the most fractured part of our house. It was also the area we found most embarrassing, the one we didn't want to show our guests. We let them imagine that *behind* the blinds hid grass, flowers, and a barbecue set up over a creek.

We'd been proud of the lawn before he came, of how evenly it grew into a flat coat of emerald green. But he clawed the whole thing up digging hidey holes, and turned our yard into a roughed-up patch of dirt. We'd put his house right in the middle. Which is why, once he was gone, his empty house was the main fracture off which all the rest of them branched—the only proof of his brief time there. Our yard had become an unattractive wasteland. The earth had cracked and taken with it all evidence that there had once been grass and in that grass flowers and *among* those flowers people who used to go outside every Sunday to sun their shoulders and make the daylight and the backyard a part of their home.

There may have been a time when we pretended the backyard belonged to someone else. We refused to look at it and tried to keep our distance. We felt every hole in the earth as if it was a profound loss, even though they looked like regular holes. Letting the eyes dwell on an absence while ignoring the surface around it is a common mistake.

With the rain and the passing days, the soil was dressed in a new layer of green and the grass threw down new roots. The ground was like a thin membrane shamelessly exposing the body's machinery. Thankfully, before it was too late, we remembered that grass clings to the surface and that its long, spread-out roots make it more resilient than other weeds. We patched the holes with fresh soil and the grass began to grow again. Over the fracture of his empty house, there is now bougainvillea. Its petals will not leave holes when they fall, but will layer over each other, one by one

Bedroom 1:1

Houses are designed to protect the private lives of the people who live in them. To reach our bedroom, you have to go through the whole house. When the sun comes up, the orange blinds that separate us from the balcony color the walls. At the foot of our bed is the rug we bought in Turkey. Our bedroom aspires to symmetry: there are two table lamps, two chairs, and two bookcases. Even though our books have almost nothing in common—on one side there's evidence of a Protestant education and on the other proof of a certain Germanophilia—I suppose there's some overlap, at least historically.

I've always wondered if a stranger walking through our house while we were out would have to go *as far as* the bedroom before realizing that two women live under this roof. Maybe the contents of our closet or our shoe size or all the fragrances in the bathroom would give us away. Maybe everyday objects reveal more than we imagine, and we can learn something about the person who inhabits them just by looking. Another me has been left somewhere. This is why there are so many series of photographs of people posing with their belongings—the trash they generate in the space of a week, homemade food—or else smiling, surrounded by objects that feel indispensable to them.

Rough-In

The first time we saw the house, it was an unfinished building with ashen walls. They handed us a pair of helmets and we walked through the roughcast construction. Every so often they reminded us to be careful with the floor or with the rods that stuck out at intimidating angles. The house's skeleton was in plain view, as were the light fixtures and cables that are now hidden behind walls. They showed us where the living room would go as well as the kitchen and the backyard, but none of it had been put in yet. We had to use our imaginations, and trust that the house would eventually exist.

MARIANA OLIVER was born in Mexico City in 1986. She received a master's degree in comparative literature from the National Autonomous University of México (UNAM) and is currently working towards a doctoral degree in modern literature at the Iberoamerican University in Mexico City. Oliver was granted a fellowship for essay writing at the Foundation for Mexican Literature and was awarded the José Vasconcelos National Young Essay Award for *Migratory Birds*.

JULIA SANCHES is a translator of Portuguese, Spanish, and Catalan. She has translated works by Susana Moreira Marques, Claudia Hernández, Daniel Galera, and Eva Baltasar, among others. Her shorter translations have appeared in various magazines and periodicals, including *Words Without Borders*, *Granta*, *Tin House*, and *Guernica*. A founding member of Cedilla & Co., Julia sits on the Council of the Authors Guild.

Undelivered Lectures is a narrative nonfiction series featuring book-length essays in slim, handsome editions.